the hispering

SARAH HYMAS

Published by Black Sunflowers Poetry Press

www.blacksunflowerspoetry.com

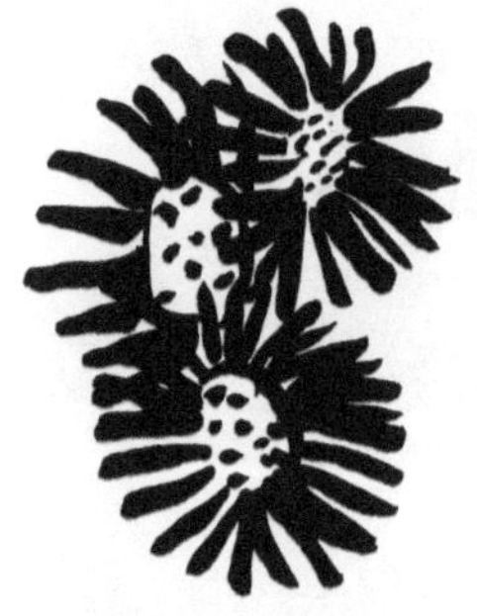

© Sarah Hymas 2021

ISBN: 978-1-8382516-3-5

TABLE OF CONTENTS

INTRO NOTE

Black Sunflowers called out and from across the globe poets answered. The cries of being and feeling were strange, funny, primal, otherworldly, and angry. Poems raged and fluttered, moaned, and muttered, soared and stumbled. From all the speakings, this voice was heard.

Enjoy,

Geffen Bankir

Amanda Holiday

Nothing more intimate, more persistent than memory lodged thirty years deep in tissue and neurons, kept alive by retelling. Each telling adding flesh, shape: layers of green on green: springtime foliage.

This dream of a meadow spreads across years, across countries, across listeners, unfolding from your memory into theirs. Dandelion and grass seeds blowing new timings into old loam.

Each account spindles on channels of moisture.

Glistening rivulets and tendrils branching, veining a way, always rooting to the ocean, however pressed flat and waveless on its journey, seeping through soil, rock, mulch, bone and plasma.

Or spray: aerosols of damp invisible and slicked bristle through fabric, air, light enough to hang on the imagination of wide- side- or dead-eyed, bated breath. You could argue a story is only animate when inhabiting its host.

You do not hoard anecdotes, and keep this story gestating through watering it only occasionally, plump on your tongue, ripened by attention. And the dreamer turns child turns dream turns seed. Because all life begins in the dark.

Store pod, soft as northern sunlight. Loose as newborn imagination. You do not want to give it a human birth. It: the dream. It: the dreamt creature

Already it ripped you from a world of certainty, as if it birthed you. Which makes you as ageless as it. There is no easy rule in a dream: no defined scale. Dream currency defies gravity. Its fallow muscle compresses in and on and over and while and here and there and no and yes and you and grasses and it and stems and spikelets and reaching and running and you and pollen and confused and assured and now and forever

and yet only today you wonder, since it gave you something, might you not have given it something back? What could you give, now you think of such an exchange?

Cells divide all the time. Light and water transform into energy. The world is in constant transaction. This for that. Photosynthesis. Respiration.

To trust enough to hold where spines are barbed and fitful, to counter the scratchiness of being on edge, to blunt the ridges that hackle. This has to be learnt through knowing fear. It could be a cure for the undiagnosed

What can you give to something you've refused, been unable, to name for the length of your lives together? The tentative suggestions you tried to brace it with only accentuate its squirming in the rough terrain of imagination and rationale, memory and control.

So you begin with another story. The story of rope. Of grasses plaited, to be braided into thicker plaits and those stitched by more grasses into longer lengths and thicker and longer until they are lines stretching sure enough to knot and ladder together and be strung over chasms, from one cliff edge to another to make a bridge upon which to cross, to continue the journey to wherever. You are not ready to be certain where, as much as you are not ready to be certain who, or what, it is.

You tried to transcribe it, not long ago, prompted by the possibility of it being something so much bigger than a thing in your head; a creature in a dream. Perhaps, rather, a thing outside you burrowing its way in, a stolon, dropped by a nesting bird, running out of sight, alive as it ever was once it contacts the humus. The trickle and fiddle of rootstalks feeding, drawing up as they draw light down. As if writing it would reveal something new.

That seeds are soft, almost liquid, when still in the pod, that sweet juice before solidifying: the spittle and sinew you share with plants before a shell hardens each casing. Just as words harden the space they disrupt.

The word you found for it was *hispering*. The forgotten
utterings that linger in meadow-traces issuing up, down, or
in. An unknown unrecognisable being or creature. The sound
of grasses swaying through grasses. Thinkings or respondings
to what is not understood.

*The hivvering needles of its winged nursery suckling sugars
riveted and wireless in chlorophyll spires.* Yes, you wrote
that, even as you knew, in the transcribing, it becomes less it,
more you. I incubate. *I creep bent and distant.*

How distinct is the grass blade from breath when pinched
between thumbs as a whistle?

To blow grass is to know the strength of its blade. An
orchestra of war grows underfoot.

I am aerial, a breeze crosshatching.

Its gift: a pointy, tendrilly pink flower you'd never seen before. A pink petalled blossoming, as if it was the stalk. Ragged robin, a cold and damp-loving flower, not so common any more. In naming comes an edge, slicing one thing from another: grass blade verge petal dream meadow sea current.

A sharp spittling to snap off and germ inside. A nursery: habitat of shelter and food. Shafts of colding light swimming in the meadow sea of dreams, where control is on a distant wavelength, reflected as blue rebounding from the water.

Your delight when you catch sight of those torn pink petals in the wild you keep to yourself. The more you tell a story the less it is something that happened, that your body feels.

Freshly cut grass emits chemicals: some stimulating new cell growth so the wounds close fast; others prevent bacterial infection; a few produce defence compounds in the as yet uncut grass, in readiness. Others attract predators higher up the food chain than the initial offender, to see off attack.

You can only believe in this cocktail from having felt the crackle white hairs bursting from each sheath, flaring in the light, fine static of antennae. Which is when you thought, with a conviction that now embarrasses you, the cosmos rises out of matted stalks.

Mind rises from the fictions of the body. Yours from childhood fairy tales. As sunlight is stored, of everything grown green. Where density seems solid. Membranes vibrate between.

Still, another tale, another interpretation:

Because what if it wasn't a hundred mattresses the princess was tested with, rather a hundred corpses? And while trying to sleep on top of the giant pile, she could still feel the pea, sprouting so far beneath, the unfurling of its stalk, despite being so thin, rippling through the layers to her hip, the lightest crackle of feathery roots searching for moisture, nutrients. Would she still be regarded as noble? Of what land?

This came as a thought more than a dream, during lockdown, in a churchyard, in an unmown area near the gate. Where only one flat gravestone was embedded in the ground. You'd gone there because of recounting the dream, again, wanting someone else to unravel the tangle of its straws and hairs, and here was a quiet, almost-meadow of tall grasses, dandelion golds and bugle flies, thousands of flies hummering, their wings catching the sunlight, and above this blackbirds and pigeons calling from the leafy streams of trees, and jackdaw chicks squabbling in the belfry. And it felt so alive you just basked in the thrum of it all. So when the church warden passed and said, 'You do know you're lying on dead bodies, don't you?' you were so bemused by her words – because obviously you did know – you didn't know what to say, so said 'Yes', and turning on that *Yes* was the image of the princess trying to sleep, or rather perhaps not trying but simply being so very awake.

What fleshing out of thought. What exchange of dream and waking. Collective runners, shooting up from the boggy earth of mind. The verge between lost and found

The hormone used to contract the womb in labour, aiding the movement of foetus to child, is the same one that passes between people when they're close physically, creating a sense of safety, fellowship. You wonder if, in times of social distancing, if it is this hormone that is secreted, in some smooth cycle of your psychic parts, through your dreams, through the arrival of others in them, sealing an intensity to their life, their pulse within yours. The same hormone can also be used to stimulate plant growth; worming its way into dreams of many stalks growing thickly, brightly. The thunder of built pressure, of hormones splitting across bodies within bodies of stories shared and yet-to-be recounted. An atmospheric hack.

You live your life submerged in light, seeing only a pinhead's worth, at half its speed.

Looking without focus through the sway of seedheads, seeing wavelengths of chlorophyll. Another breath and you could tip into the Atlantic.

You only prioritise waking over dream because of those around you.

Otherwise you might be persuaded that the universe has folded itself into something you cannot grasp, that has held you, will hold you for twenty, thirty, forty more years. And each time you tell it, you reassemble the meadow ocean inside out.

Because who's to say the dream meadow was not a sea meadow, grasses immersed in air the way you are in water. Plant brain, like octopus brain, is a decentralised system, an embodied receptor. The smallest blade of grass, the thinnest ligule, is its rudder.

That afternoon I was walking a dog around the lanes around the camp, and realised halfway my hat was no longer on my head. I dithered over whether to go back and look for it, or go, oh well, I've lost my hat, and walk on. But it was a hat I'd made, out of silk, so I decided to try and find it. I didn't have to go very far back. It was bright red, less than five minutes behind us, arresting in the vegetation. I picked it up. And underneath was a cluster of flowers – the flowers the creature had offered me in my dreaming just that morning, ones I'd never seen before that day, and now, in real life in inverted commas, they were right in front of me, growing their pinky-tissued star-shaped pointy petals in the thick ferny verge.

Some months later, I was in north west Ireland, at a camp where a woman was offering a dream workshop. I'd never been to anything like that before, or since. I joined the group as she was asking for a volunteer and barged my hand up immediately. I knew exactly which dream I wanted to return to.

She guided me back to the meadow and the creature was there, still hunched, and this time I was calm. I was facing it, its pointy sappy green hand reaching towards me crouching like it. The thinnest slither between us. And I saw what it was holding in its palm. I didn't take the flower. I just saw it, and knew enough for the daydreaming to be over.

The Story

A long time ago I had a dream of lying in a meadow, among tall glissing grasses, looking up at blue sky in that delightfully uneventful dreamlike way. After a dreamlength period of time I became aware of a rustling – a presence behind me. It was as though I was dreaming within the dream. I squinted over my right shoulder and this creature was squatting – large-ish, the size of a small adult, but no higher than the grasses around us. Everything about it was pointy and sallow. If it had stood up it could well have been much taller than me. But it didn't. It was murmuring something I didn't understand. As the voice became more urgent, sharper, stitching into the breezy grasses, prickling my skin, the creature reached its hand towards me. Long tapering fingers closer and closer, slightly curled as if holding something in its palm. I was so shocked – at its proximity, its appearance, its sound, its nearing me – I woke myself up.

I couldn't turn back to sleep. That was that. That was the dream. And I was awake.

Author Acknowledgements

the hispering grew from this story under the attentive care of Steve Lewis and Sally Slade Payne during the spring of 2020. Thanks, too, to Helen Tookey who, as ever, encouraged and inspired.

Black Sunflowers Poetry Press

Backed by an array of artists, activists, poets and poetry fans from all walks of life, Black Sunflowers, the UK's first crowdfunded poetry press, came into being in March 2020 with a pledge to publish and promote the work of women, older women and black poets from the UK and around the world. Black Sunflowers is grateful to Nat West's #BackHerBusiness scheme, all the supporters including Patrick Bill, Amanda Sebestyen, Cathy Greenhalgh, Rehana Zaman, Rob Curry, Nadine Marsh-Edwards, Rosa Fong, Judah Attille, Elinor Perry-Smith, Monika Baker, David Curtis, Oona Hyland, Janice Cheddie, Simone Alexander, Mustapha Feika, Michael Cadette and others who wish to remain anonymous, as well as the additional enterprise finance awarded to us. Black Sunflowers is thankful to those who have offered encouragement and advice along the way and who have contributed their skills or inspired through their own publishing entrepreneurship.

Embarking on this venture during Covid19, on the cusp of a lockdown, was challenging and perhaps folly. Yet, with daily life on hold, this has been a time for deep reflection for all of us. A time perhaps to pause for poetry.